Top Money Making Strategies

**(A Powerful Guide to Using Six Online
Services for Your Financial Independence)**

BASSEY JIMMY

ISBN: 11546830375
ISBN-13: 978-1546830375

DEDICATION

This book is dedicated to the Almighty God for His love and wisdom that has overwhelmed me and leads me in putting this piece of work together.

CONTENTS

ACKNOWLEDGMENTS

I am grateful to my friend, Wisdom who has helped in contributing as well as proof reading of this book itself.

I feel a deep sense of gratitude to my precious wife, Esther, and our children, Dominion, Blessing, Rhema and Joy for their patience and support from conception of this book to its present form. You are a gift to me, and may your gift continue to make a way for you in the world.

INTRODUCTION

I'd like you to know that **"Money Making Strategies For Today"** book is authentic and real, just as the name implies.

I'm really excited about this book because it seems everyone is interested in making money online as it is the simplest thing to do nowadays out of the Nine-To-Five job. If you search on Google on ways to make money online or browse your favorite online marketing forum for a few minutes, you will be amazed at the thousands of searches and questions on this topic.

To help those who are new online and are really interested in making money online, I decided to put together in this Book, the different ways of making money online. This Book will expose to you the simple step-by-step guide to gaining your financial freedom through six evergreen online services.

There is money everywhere but people don't just know where to find it. This book will take you through the intricacies of internet marketing to discovering where and how to get the pie.

Let's get started.

1 CHAPTER ONE

Blogging for Money

Blogging is a cost-effective source of making profit. Blogs are simple and uncomplicated to set up, manage and maintain. With blogging, you write what you love and whenever you feel like doing, this is wonderful. The sheer flexibility of blogging makes it lighter and easier for you to just sit back, relax and go on a vacation whenever you feel like it while money flows into your account.

In this step, we are going to look into the profitability of a blog and how to set up a blog of our own at no cost! That sounds interesting!

To start with this, we need to obtain a blog. Many options exist for owning a blog; you can create a blog on your own domain or you register for free blog on google blogging platform. For starters, let's talk about the free blogs. You can obtain a free blog at www.blogger.com or the newer (and better), www.wordpress.com.

Blogger.com is a free host by Google and having a blog though cheaper will not give you all the features you need. But Wordpress is preferred because of its many options and features which makes it very simple to understand even by newbies. Therefore, Wordpress is better in the sense that it has more advanced features such as Track back and Categories.

How to Get Started in Blogging

This tutorial is going to help you put up your blog without problems. You just need to follow this guide and make sure you don't omit any of the steps.

To start blogging you need to do these two important things. These are outlined below:

1. Make Sure to pick a domain name.

You can customize your domain name to any name of your choice for your online business. It may be your name or something close to your business.

Domain name is your identity. A Good blog name should be descriptive and unique. This is what your audience will easily use to identify what your blog is about. You may decide to use your name. Top bloggers use their names as domain name. This helps prevent someone else from registering your name.

Write down some blog name ideas and choose a domain name extension. Most people use .com extension because it is the standard. Try to avoid other extensions like .us or .net since people are not really familiar with those. If your domain name is taken, you may add simple words like "a", or "the" to the beginning of the name.

2. Choose a web host.

The next step is to choose a web host. This is a company that specializes in storing your data and information for your blog if you want to host your site with them. Without a web host, you can't have a blog.

It is your web host that determines how your blog will be. If you go for a bad host, your business is doomed even before you start. There are numerous web host companies you can choose from among which I recommend you use either Hostgator.com or blueHost.com for your blog. These web host companies are reliable, uptime is perfect and their customer service is excellent.

How to set up your Blog

For the purpose of following this ebook, I have decided to use BlueHost web host for this tutorials.

1. Follow this link http://bluehost.com to get started now".

2. Select the plan of your choice. I recommend the basic plan for you if you are new to online marketing. Otherwise, click "Select" to choose your preferred plan.

3. Type in your domain name in the left box and then click "next" to see if it is available.

If you already own a registered domain name and want to use it for your blog, type your existing domain name in the right box and then click "next". Only use the right box if you have a registered domain!

4. To get a domain name, you can register a name and if it is not available, domain names similar to yours will be made available for you to choose from. You can choose any of the suggested domains or type in another name.

5. You will be taken to registration page once you have found an available domain name. You will then be asked for your billing details.

6. Next is to fill in your choice hosting package among three options.

7. An option will be given to you to create a password for your account. A blog will automatically be installed when you have done that. Next, a page should come up with this message; Click "Log into WordPress" to be taken to your blog.

Your log-in details will be sent to your email.

Know that the login details for your blog are not the same as your BlueHost account. Make sure to keep track of this information.

How to Use Your Blog

Once you have successfully installed WordPress on your site you are ready to start blogging.

Below are basic steps you need to follow to get your blog up and running.

Logging In

To begin, you will need to login to your site. Go to http://www.yoursite.com/wp-admin to bring up the login screen. Next, replace "yoursite.com" with your registered domain name). If you are unsure of your login name or password, go to your email box and check the log in details that was sent to you from BlueHost that has this information.

Changing Your Blog Title

You will be taken to administrator area after you logged in to your Wordpress account. You can make changes here and you need to start with your blog title. To do this, move to the bottom of the left menu and click on Settings.

After the changes, you can start writing.

Blogging and Affiliate Products Promotion

A blog is a powerful tool for making money online with affiliate marketing. A blog is not only a marketing tool for your affiliate programs; it's also your brand name or your business platform.

Therefore, you must spend some time to learn writing good blog posts that will pre-sell your affiliate products. You make affiliate sales because of your suggestions and convincing words, and the readers are motivated by your suggestions and recommendations.

For ultimate results, let your blog posts be what your audience need. Let it create value to them and likewise, they will buy from you. A poor blog post can annoy the readers and drive them away from your blog.

To make your blog really work for you, you really need to write good marketing blog post often. So, it is suggested you sign up for some writing courses to improve your business writing skills. You are going to need to concentrate on web writing and creative writing. You must put in time and effort to master the fields of marketing and writing. Only then you will be able to write compelling blog posts that will capture your readers' attention, while promoting your affiliate product through the blog.

You can hire an experienced freelance writer to write quality posts for you.. Tell the writer what affiliate products or services you want to promote and he will do the research and write blog contents that will interest your readers while marketing your affiliate programs in a smooth way.

Make sure inside every marketing posts have the relevant associate text links included. Your interesting blog content will persuade readers to click on your affiliate links to visit the sale page of your affiliate products.

Doing affiliate marketing is much like building a home based business. Good result wouldn't come instantly. More effort and hard work must be put in before you can see the good result you dream of. As you are using a blog for associate marketing, you must regularly and persistently be publishing interesting and informative blog posts in order to create trust and credibility within your readers.

Tips on Promoting Your Blog

Most people fail when it comes to promoting their blogs. They don't know how to go about it even though they are great bloggers.

Don't let anything prevent you from showcasing your work. Promoting your blog will give you confidence as well as help you to put more effort in making your work stand out.

I have listed below the different ways of promoting your blog and it's absolutely free.

1. Email marketing

2. Social networks

3. Commenting on other blogs

4. Link to other blogs

5. Guest posting

6. Online forums

7. Frequent posting

Steps on How to Monetize your Blog

To get the best out of your blog, you'll need to;

1. Have knowledge already (or you will have to research).

2. Enjoy writing on the subject.

So, go and write your first post. Don't worry about your chosen affiliate product yet.

Below are some pointers to note when you are writing posts;

1. **Make it readable.** You want your readers to stick around, so do not post non-stop promotions on your blog.

2. **Write in your own way**. Your new blog is an indication of your thoughts and proficiency. Don't try and pretend to be something you're not. Remember that you are writing about a subject you are passionate about – so just be yourself.

3. **Encourage your readers to post comments**. Search engines love new and fresh content, and the easiest way to get this is through your blog readers.

4. **When you have a few posts on your blog, you can start to slowly and cautiously promote your affiliate product.**

5. **Don't make it to obvious that you are trying to make money**. Simply provide the odd link within your content. This is where many bloggers get it wrong.

6. **Refinement is the key here**. Remember, it's more imperative to focus on good content that will keep your visitors on your blog longer and look for ways of encouraging them to come back in the future.

So, how do you go about starting a blog that you can make money online per month?

An overview of the process goes thus:

1) Look for a need of your audience.

Get answers to the problems and needs of your audience

2) Research the competition.

Follow your competitors, see what they do and how they interact with their customers. Then build and set your blog with the information gathered and make it better.

3) Visit WordPress.org, install and customize your blog the way you want.

4) Start blogging! As you are starting, fill your blog with about ten posts, just to make sure your early visitors get the feeling that you have a popular blog with good contents. Then make it necessary to update your blog at least two or three times a month. If possible, you can even be updating it daily.

You can pre-load content and "drip" it to your readers on a pre-set schedule. You can do this by either loading up the content and setting it for a future posting date, or by purchasing auto-blogging software that will do all the work for you.

Here's what you need to know to start driving traffic to your blog and make money sooner:

2 CHAPTER TWO

Article Writing That Sells

If you want to make money online, you can create and sell your own information products. Information product is never out of stock as long as people are having problems. Information product is basically providing answers, directives, guides, reports, tips to day by day problems people encounter at home, work place, businesses, health as well as services that need to be provided.

And the best way to package information marketing is through article writing. Can you write? Can you create humour? Do you have answers to most problems people encounter on a daily basis? If your answer to any of these questions is Yes, then, you can begin from here.

You just have to look inside of you and bring it out. It could be that:

- • You know how to manage the family budget.
- • You could teach others how to create and sell DIY (Do-it-yourself) stuff.
- • You know how to gain and loss weight effortlessly.
- • You know how breed and raise dogs, rabbit etc.
- • You know how to handle and overcome stress easily.

The above list includes just six ideas... but you can add more!

Tips for Article Writing

Take time to brainstorm your interests and talents, and you'll quickly realize that you know a lot about a particular subject.

Once you have figured out what to write about, carefully apply the following steps on the entire process.

1) Research the competition and use it to develop a better product.

Now, you don't want to present to your market the exact product your competitors are giving to the customers. You, on the other hand should make your product unique and better. So your next step is to research the competitors' products to determine how you can perk up upon the products the market is already buying.

2) Create the product. After that, take action.

Sketch out an outline and set a target of writing XXXX words per day. If creating the product doesn't sound like something you want to do yourself, then you can outsource the task.

3) Set up your website, including a lead-capture system.

Next, you need to write a sales letter that will pre-sell your eBook. Next is to upload it to a web page. You will also set up a squeeze page with an auto responder as a means to get your visitors to join your newsletter list.

4) Set up your backend sales system.

It's not a difficult process. Certainly, you can stream it down to a few words: **Find a hungry market and give them what they want.**

3 CHAPTER THREE

Profiting With EBay

EBay is a marketplace where different kinds of products ranging from watches to cars are advertised for buyers and sellers. There are many people who make their living from selling on EBay and I know you too can!

And anyone who is browsing eBay is likely planning on buying something, which means almost everyone who looks at your ad, will be a person who already has their credit card out. You'd be hard pressed to find "hotter" leads than the people browsing eBay!

There are plenty of ways of getting these people browsing eBay. But in general, you'll likely use one of two models:

a) Using eBay firmly as a lead generator.

Have you ever wonder why would someone choose to lose money on eBay?

It's simple - because they're using eBay as a lead generator. That means they are selling low-cost products to pull people into their sales funnel. Once the buyers are in their sales funnel, then the marketer works to sell them more products and more expensive products through email or newsletters.

b) Using eBay directly to pull in profit.

The method you choose depends on what you're selling. If you're selling something like antiques, you may find you get higher prices by putting them on the auction block rather than by offering them for a fixed price to your customer list.

What do you need to sell on eBay?

For you to succeed on eBay, you need to choose a hungry niche (what people are really looking for) and focus entirely on that one niche.

Once you find the hungry niche, find out what the customers are buying and start giving it to them.

You can create your own products or look for products that will give you resell rights to market.

Steps to take before selling on eBay

To get you started on this platform, follow the step by step guide below:

First You Must Sign up or Sign In!

The first and basic step is to sign up so you can have access to Ebay marketplace.

Creating a Listing on Ebay

Know that on eBay portal, listing products is completely free. Therefore, you create a listing of what you want to sell on eBay and give it a good description. Make sure that your description will give your potential buyers a good mental image of your listed item as they go through it.

Highlighting the main features of the item is vital as they will be attracted to the product. Use good brand names when doing so.

Take as many as possible great photos of the product from different angles so that buyers may see what they will be buying. Adding up to 12 free photos gives you an edge over other sellers.

In online marketing, buyers always want to see what they are buying. Make it a duty to take pictures that will 'sell' your product. Always remember that photos are of vital important to your prospective buyers and can make or mar a sale.

Choose your Price

Pricing in eBay is a very sensitive issue as setting a price that buyers think is low, may make them think that your product is of low quality. In the other way round, potential buyers may be scared if your price is high.

To run an auction, the best time to do so is on weekends.

Make a little to know the market value for your item, and then select the fixed price listing format. Only use the auction-style listing format if you have special or unique items, or when the value of the item is not known.

Choose How You Want To Ship Products

When you finish setting the price of your product, the next step is to choose a shipment method. Shipping is a great way to offer customer service and build your reputation in the eBay marketplace. This occurs after the buyer has paid for your product. You will need to ensure that the package is safe for shipping and delivery.

You can get shipping supplies ahead of time on My eBay. EBay works with all major couriers for simple shipping. Because of this, you are guaranteed great rates

There are three options for shipping to buyers namely; the flat rate option, the calculated shipping option and the local pick-up option. You have the option of choosing either free shipping or international shipping. International shipping gives you a wider reach and a wider market, across different parts of the world.

Always go for minimal shipping charges as best as you can. Be sure that your shipping option gets the package to the buyer in good condition. Furthermore, the package should reach the buyer within or on the specified date stated when shipping. The happy buyer will give you a positive feedback if you deliver the products on time and on good condition. This will potentially sky rock your sales.

Getting paid on EBay

Your money is send immediately to Paypal once your item has been sent to the buyer. This makes it so easy. Also, you get paid faster if you use the eBay shipping labels and receive payments with PayPal. PayPal is the fastest and most secure way to get paid for sold listings on eBay.

Important tips on selling on EBay

1. Use really good pictures for listing your items. Make sure the pictures are not blurred.

2. Take time to write out compelling descriptions of the items you are listing. When writing description, think about potential buyers.

3. Do your market research well. Go for items that are popular and you are convinced will really sell without 30 days.

4. Time your listing right and avoid reserve prices

5. Choose what to sell carefully and avoid competition.

4 CHAPTER FOUR

Craigslist Profits

It's very astonishing to know that even though people think it is not possible, you can earn a living from Craigslist. People are starting to understand the different opportunities you can exploit to make money on the portal if you decide to work hard.

For someone just starting out, you need to know the basics of Craigslist's marketplace and how to get going on the site without hitches. You need to know how project yourself and your services to the visitors of the site, and get those interested in your products to buy without hesitation.

With Craigslist, you have no need to worry about promoting your products and services. All you need do is advertise and you will be contacted by both offline and online buyers who are interested in your products. There are 2 ways you can earn a living through Craigslist. You may decide to offer your services or products in the following ways:-
As a freelance or as a stand alone contractor who provides your services to a customer on an agreement basis.

You may offer your products or services to others as a business owner would.

Profitable Craigslist Business Model

There are so many things one should know about Craigslist if one plan to sell something on the site. The beautiful things about Craigslist are its user-friendliness, and free option of listing of products to be sold on the site.

Proper Market Research

Proper market research is important because it will help you to identify product popularity as well as its competition. With market research, you can easily know the probabilities of your products being sold. This exercise doesn't take time. It's important you do these things if your plan is to sell products on the site.

Sometimes you need to exercise patient if your item is not popular, until there is an upsurge demand for it.

Other vital information you need to note when doing market research on

Craigslist are:

• Pricing for other items

• Description of other items

• How these are different or relate to your item

Describe your Item in and out

You need to have a quality description of your item as this will physically describe it when you are not there. Make sure your descriptions meet the questions you may have from your customers. Such questions may include but not limited to:

• What is your product?

• Are there any problems in it?

• Are any items missing?

• Is it used or new?

Make sure the information you provide are the same you may be looking for when purchasing that item.

You can include the following basic and vital information:

• Model of Item

• Make

• Brand

• Age

• Add-ons

• Malfunctions

• Issues

• And any other information you may feel should be shared with the buyers. Note that sellers with poor descriptions hardly sell their products.

Display Good Photographs

Photos are very important tools on Craigslist as there are essential and a remarkable way to increase your sales. It is good if you upload multiple images of each listing on Craigslist. Make sure you have at least one image for your listing, irrespective of the product.

With great photographs, you can sell your products easily. Have it at the back of your mind that, good pictures bring good sales, while terrible ones may not even bring a sale.

Highlight Competition

Nowadays, people are price conscious and Craigslist gets benefited naturally when people buy consistently from the site. All the deals on Craigslist are just about exchanging. A seller gives the best price and in turn a buyer would offer their counter price.

To stay in competition is the key point and for that to happen you need to always keep a watch on your competitors taking into cognizance:

• What is the cost of their item?

• Are you quoting higher than them?

• If their cost is less, why?

To sell your products quickly, the price you advertise would be a major deciding factor. You can decide to start high and then go low. By doing so, you would have the chance to bargain.

Give Prompt Reply

Never keep your prospective buyers waiting for answers to their queries. Doing so is considered rude.

Reselling the Freebies available on Craigslist

You might have used Craigslist consistently to sell or buy things, but wouldn't have ever realized that there are people who give away freebies on this site. There is a section specifically dedicated to this option, "Free." People just give away their things for free, because it is many times easier to get rid of them this way as compared to taking the time to sell them. However, it is not always so hard to sell such items, you just need to learn the art of selling and you can earn in thousands by selling those items you get for free.

How to locate free items?

• Check your local directory for listing. On reaching the local directory, under "For Sale" section, click "free" link

Here you will see Ads for almost everything, few examples are:

• Leftovers from a sale

• Windows

• Wood doors

• Sliding doors

• Refrigerator

• Hot tub

- Bathroom countertop

- Toilet seat

- Firewood

- Artificial Christmas tree

- Full size functional trampoline

- Television

Collect all items which are in good condition as you check the description and images of the listed items. The trick here is to list back the items you get free on the site as soon as you possibly can. Anything you earn in this way would be a clear profit.

How to resell these freebies?

There are different ways to sell the free items that you picked on Craigslist, you may decide to:

1. Resell on Craigslist

2. Sell to specific buyers

The first option is a clear example of flipping where you are capitalizing on the market inefficiencies. Free is the lowest form of cheap, and "another place" would just be a different Ad category that is not free.

If you are planning to opt for this option, you should have a list prepared for the best places you sold an item to. This list can include:

• Metal buyers (for copper and aluminum items),

• Pawn shops (tools, luggage, jewelry and electronics),

• Buyers for used appliance

• Old furniture buyers

• Consignment shops,

• A bookstore that is willing to purchase old and used books.

Most Profitable Items on Craigslist

Items which are priced higher, and with adequate supplies, are the best products to sell and buy on the site.

Why products which are high priced?

Items priced higher give an opportunity to earn more profit as compared to low priced products; supposing that the amount of total work required is same.

However on the flip side, when you purchase high priced products, your chances for loss also increase.

Sufficient supply: What does it mean?

Here you have enough quantity of items to sell or buy, and make desirable profits. Considering all the factors mentioned above, the following items can be considered as the top ten items that are on greater demand on Craigslist.

1. Four wheelers, especially Cars

Try and bargain for a good deal with cars because they usually have a huge profit margin. Depending on the age, condition, make and type, a car will range from $5000 - $10000. A car you buy at half price and given a few repair jobs can earn you a couple grand within days.

2. Power equipment and tools

There is a large supply of Power apparatus, tools and equipment when dealers change professions and put all their equipment on Craigslist.

3. Yard tools

Generators, power washers, chainsaws, weed eaters, chippers/shredders, leaf blowers and lawnmowers. Most people abandoned their tools and equipment with gas in it during the winter season which can lead to carburetor clogging.

4. Computers

Computers and laptops if repaired can bring you huge amount of profits. When the computers have some fault, people just drop them off at cheaper price on Craigslist.

5. Electronic items

High-end electronic items can be sold at a good price. There are many subcategories that vary in electronic field. Sometimes, people purchase items without even thinking; soon they get rid of it after hardly using it. These items can be stored in the house while waiting for them to be sold out.

6. Furniture

Furnishings are very costly, mostly high-end furniture. Solid wood furniture is in high demand. Beds, all types of chairs, dining tables, desks, mirrors, nice couch. Take advantage of this if you want to make more profit.

7. Bikes

One can earn a good amount of money in reselling and buying of bicycles. After a few repairs, the value of a bike can increase drastically.

8. Mobile Phones

Mobile Phones, especially new smart phones are being sold at good prices in the used item markets. People always upgrade their phones, therefore making the supply large. The demand here is bigger because it is expensive to replace a broken or lost phone. The mobile phone market is inefficient in the sense that people get their mobile phones by their carrier provider; hence its actual cost is hidden from its real holder.

9. Motorbikes and Scooters

You can make good money by buying and selling of motorbikes and scooters. You can buy the bikes and scooters at a very cheap price in winters and sell them at higher price in summers.

10. Electrical device

We all use electric device and appliances at home. The demand and supply for electrical appliances is pretty high. It's quite easy to make good profit per appliance, especially more in the high-end electronic devices.

How to Find Profitable Items to Sell

You need to focus on the products which have good demand and supply and even better profit margins. Appliances can be the best bid here.

Supply

This is the most significant aspect as you need something which keeps you going for a whole year. People always change their preferences, tastes and also have the need to go for upgrades; so appliances always have enough supply. Even the appliance of lowest level can be sold here.

Demand

There is an increased demand for used appliances day-by-day on Craigslist; as people can now purchase them in much lower cost (1/4th to 1/3rd) than the new ones. This can help them save a lot of money.

High Quality Products

Constant selling and buying from Craigslist will help you discover models and brands that are of good quality, and can easily get you good profits as well.

How to Sell Your Items Fast on Craigslist

The following tips should guide you if you want to sell items fast and earn amazing profits:

1. Set a price that is realistic.

While setting the price, keep in mind that irrespective of the condition of your product, unused, box-packed or new, you would not get the complete price. The one guarantee that your product is sold quickly is its reasonable price. Few things you should consider while setting the price of your product can be:

• What would be the cost of this item in garage sales?

• Check the demand of product you are planning to sell.

After considering all the aforementioned pointers you would be able to set an appropriate price.

2. Provide a detailed description of the item.

As mentioned earlier, a quality description is something which works when you are not there to physically describe your item. All the details specified in this book would give wings to your product. When you provide less information, you are likely to see few email requests. It is through your description that prospective buyers will take decisions

3. Sell your item to the first buyer with cash in hand.

You should remember that your reason for being on this site is to sell and earn profits and not to socialize. Therefore, you have the freedom of being disloyal to prospective buyers. Rather than giving priority to someone who emailed you first, you may scan all your emails and may give it to someone who can pick it first. In this way you would have your cash and buyer would have his product in no time. This would also ensure that you are not holding the product for such a long time for someone who is indecisive.

Creating Craigslist Advert

A well prepared Craigslist Advert would make sure that the item you are listing is sold faster and at a high price. A nicely prepared advert would make the entire experience pleasant for you and the buyer.

1. Write great headlines that capture the buyer's attention

The title should be short and straight to the point. Have accurate title with short precise details.

2. Great photographs

The background should be clean and free of mess. Make sure the pictures are taken in a well lit place. Avoid close-up pictures with high resolution.

3. Detailed descriptions

These are what should not be included in your description: Does the item work without any issues? Is something not working properly? Does it require cleaning? Can the product be seen before purchase? These should not be a part of description?

How to Close the Deal with the Buyer and Seller

As a Seller:

You should be fast in replying to the queries of prospective buyers.

Fast response to phone calls especially those that landed in your voicemail.

As a Buyer:

Be smart and get in touch with the seller as soon as possible, if you like the product.

Once the deal is finalized, try to buy the product at the earliest possible time and create a meeting with the seller.

Tips for Buying & Selling on Craigslist

Before you can start on Craigslist it is important to know that there are some bad people in the world. While posting or purchasing on Craigslist, make sure that you follow these basic instructions:

Do not post your address: You may send your address to the concerned person who will be making the final purchase, but do not post your address on the listing itself as this may attract many people to your home.

Be smart: If you are a beautiful woman who is alone at home, do not tell the guy that is purchasing your laptop to come over. Meet him at a Store or at the local park which is a public place. Do not place yourself in a private place with a stranger. If the location is not safe, move out as soon as you possibly can.

If you cannot meet in public, be careful: Many people are uncomfortable in coming to someone else's house. For both parties to benefit, you may set up the meeting at a common public place.

The following tips will help you avoid any unwanted incident:

1. Never inform your apartment number. Just provide your address and first meet the person outside.

Don't close your door at the time of sale. This would ensure that you are heard in case you are in some problem.

2. Find either a friend or relative to be with you at the time of sale. If it happens you are alone try to be online with someone.

Use Google Voice in place of your phone number: Using Google voice number is the most advisable option for Craigslist marketing. The numbers provided to you have an auto router that is set up to your current mobile number. You can block them if you start getting unwanted calls. It is the easiest way to safe guard your privacy.

Secrets of Successful Craigslist Sellers

I believe you might have used Craigslist before for one thing or the other. You either had something to sell or buy. I have compiled these tips which I know will give you the desirable results. These strategies are what top Craigslist sellers are using to turn huge profit off of this platform. Applying these strategies to your Craigslist business will make a huge difference.

1. Repost your Ad to keep it on Top

Buyers are never interested to scroll through the pages to search for the old posts. Don't wait for another 30 days to post your ad as it would consume time for its purchase. Therefore, if you don't receive a response within 7 days, consider reposting it. As soon as your ads are posted, it would reflect on top of the selected category.

2. Good Image is the KEY

We all like pictures and are easily moved by captivating photos. Therefore, it is advisable to post a good image if you are planning to sell something.

Most times ads are rejected because there is no image or the images are of poor quality.

3. Avoid putting a question in your title.

Questions should be avoided on title of ads for a tangible product as it may leave an impression that the ad has been posted by a salesman or a dealer.

4. Be Specific

While posting an ad, be specific, do go beyond and do not stay behind. You should refrain from giving out too many details. Have in mind that on Craigslist first impression is everything.

5. Do proper research

This site has hundreds of products that are posted on it every day. Do a market research on products you want to sell if you want to outsmart your competitors, taking into account their pricing, condition, posting age. Identify the reason it's still not being sold. All these information would help you create a convincing ad.

6. Respond Swiftly

As a seller, be fast in replying to the emails or calls. This leaves a good impression in the mind of buyers and they would start considering buying your product. If there is a delay in your response, buyers won't hold on for long but would jump to next available item.

7. Trading can also be an option

Barter system is still alive on Craigslist. There are many people who are selling something and on other hand looking out for something. You may mention the availability of this option as well.

The above 7 steps would help your items to sell quickly. Last but not the least....Do not forget to remove the listings as soon as they sold out.

5 CHAPTER FIVE

Take Advantage of YouTube

YouTube is the most ground-breaking and one of the easiest ways to make money online. YouTube has become tremendously accepted in the last few years, in respects to the amount of traffic that any website receives on the internet.

YouTube is presently the third largest website in the world, just after Facebook. And no-one is taking advantage of this big opportunity. One thing I can guarantee you is that you are going to be among the lucky people that are making money with YouTube.

With YouTube, I am going to show you how to use a niche and target all of the highest ranking and most viewed "authority" videos on **YouTube**, and placing your links, straight in there. It is as simple as that! Then the money starts rolling in.

Now, if you're a complete newbie to the whole internet promotion scene, then don't worry, because I guarantee you after ready this, you will know everything you need to know about YouTube online marketing strategy.

YouTube and Affiliate Marketing?

As I earlier mentioned, online affiliate marketing is the easiest and very effective method of making a living online.

Remember, affiliate marketing is when you become an associate of somebody else's product, and they pay you commission when you make sales. You can easily find available products on an online "marketplace" such as http://www.clickbank.com or http://www.markethealth.com but these are only two of the many markets. There will always be a market for every niche.

When you sign up as an affiliate and you are ready to promote a product, affiliate links are given to you by the marketplace, for example, Clickbank, and are used to track a sale made by you, and exactly how many sales you make. They are an very useful part of your business, and will make up all of your links that you will use when promoting your selected product.

Why YouTube Then?

Since YouTube is one of the biggest growing advertising opportunities, and people are discovering fame overnight on YouTube, it is therefore important that you use this massive social tool, and take a slice of all those visitors floating around.

There are videos on YouTube that have thousands, sometimes up to millions of views in a few days when uploaded to the internet. To make money, you need to embed your affiliate link into any of those videos.

Steps on creating a Youtube channel

1. Sign up for a YouTube account by clicking the "Sign Up" button in the

upper-right hand corner of the site. You may want to create a special email account that is connected to your YouTube account so multiple users can have access to it.

2. Once you've registered, login to your account: **http://youtube.com/login**

3. Click on the "My Account" link.

Features of Youtube channel

We'll walk you through the following easy-to-use features on your YouTube channel:

• Profile Information

• Branding on Channel & Watch Pages

• Channel Background Image

• Featuring Videos

Channel Info

1. In "My Account" click on "Channel Info". Fill in the "Title" and Description" fields.

2. In "My Account" click on "Profile Setup" and add personal information to your profile - also use this space to tell people why you're on YouTube.

Channel Banner

1. In "My Account" click on "Edit Channel" and then click on the "Branding

Options" link.

2. Upload your banner graphic, sized 960 x 150 (or smaller), in the "Channel Banner" section.

3. Be sure to incorporate a URL that will link your banner back to us– we suggest linking back to your .gov site.

Having a channel banner makes your channel page stands out.

Branding Options

A still frame from one of your videos is used as your channel icon. You can set up the thumbnail of any selected video as your icon. The "Video Page Banner" sits on video "watch pages" and helps viewers return to your channel by clicking the graphic.

1. In "My Account" click on "Edit Channel" and then click on the "Branding Options" link.

2. Make sure you scroll down to each branding option on the page and note the required pixel-sized graphic. Then upload your image to specifications.

How to Customize your Channel Background

To personalize the background image of your channel:

1. In "My Account" click on "Edit Channel" and go to "Channel Design".

2. Under "Advanced Design Customization," add a URL that contains the image you'd like to upload.

3. You can also choose to repeat an uploaded image by opting-in to, "Repeat

Background Image".

Channel Featured Video

You should highlight one of your best videos to auto-play when someone comes to your channel.

1. In "My Account" click on "Channel Design" found in the "Edit Channel" module.

2. Under "Featured Video" you will have the choice of entering a video URL (from any YouTube channel) or setting your channel to automatically feature your latest video.

How to create Playlists

Think of Playlists as packaging your videos into different categories. How are your videos related?

1. Go to the "My Account" page and click on the "Videos, Favorites, and playlists" link.

2. Click the "New" button and set the properties (title, description, etc.) for your new Playlist.

3. Click the "Save Changes" button. You'll be returned to the "My Playlists" page and can begin adding videos.

4. When you find a video on YouTube that you want to add to the playlist, click on the "Playlists" button and select which playlist you'd like to add the video to.

How to Upload a video on Youtube

1. Click on the yellow "upload" button on the upper right corner of any YouTube watch page.

2. Upload your video file - any video format should work, just make sure it is under 1.0 Gigabytes.

3. Enter in all the relevant information about your video in the title, tags, and description so that when people search YouTube, they can find it.

This step is very important - a lot of people find videos on YouTube by sing search.

Tips to get you started on YouTube

1. Do a Thorough Research: Find out what your competitors, subscribers and the general public are saying about important events and happenings.

2. Flood the system: People are always searching for information on you, and on the topics or niches you care about. Let people see what interest them on your YouTube channel.

3. Instant Messaging: So much of your YouTube traffic comes from daily search, so post quality information of the events of the day online so people can find it.

4. Crisis Messaging: Messages that damage your online reputation will grow if not attended to immediately.

5. Message Testing: YouTube is a free focus group. Reply to comments to see how your message is resonating.

6. Engage Your Constituents: YouTube is a two-way communication tool.

Don't fail to interact with your subscribers.

Steps to Making Money on YouTube

To succeed and make money from YouTube, you need to carry out a lot of research for information, know what you want to achieve and how to easily get a slice off the millions of visitors to the site with your own technique. I have compiled for you a quicker way of breaking into YouTube profits.

Go for a profitable niche

A profitable niche is a niche you can turn into money. There are many niches to choose from. But you must remember this has to be a niche that is going to make you money, after all, that's what you are here for.

The niches that will make you money any day, any time are the most profitable things like, weight loss, skin products (acne, anti aging etc.), muscle building and self help. And it's easy to see why selling stuff is very easy.

Sourcing for YouTube Videos.

To start looking for videos, search on YouTube for videos with keywords related to your niche, for example, my niche is muscle building, I would look for "muscle building," "exercise routine," "workout" etc. It is that easy! And that is what this system is all about, if you follow my technique attentively.

When searching for videos researched and get your hands on a video or videos that has:

- •• High view count.
- •• Short upload time.
- •• Active.
- •• Related to your niche.

You need to get permission from the video's owner to use his video and also agree his payment terms. You can decide to pay them either a one off fee or by a monthly basis.

You can also create your own videos for using free video creating software and upload same to YouTube.

Cloak your affiliate link

You need to cloak or shortened your affiliate link before embedding it into your video. The most used shortener is free. You can easily operate it to use with your videos. You can get it from http://www.bit.ly. You should sign up for an account here, the tool allows you turn your affiliate link into a much shorter, neater link, and it will also track how many times your link is clicked!

There are other link shorteners though. Google for it and use the one you are conversant with. It can dramatically improve your click through rate. So this is a must for your affiliate links.

Now if you are an experienced online marketer already, I don't have any doubt that you will see the profits that this system can have to your online business. If you have a website already, you will use this method to drive traffic to your built websites or products. You don't even need niche relevant videos because if you get a link visible to 10,000 people a day you are going to get visitors to your site.

Evidently, now you have seen that this is a very EASY and SIMPLE system, and knowing how it works, I believe you will not leave any stone unturned to boosting your online business.

6 CHAPTER SIX

Fiverr Money Secrets

Fiverr is a top marketplace which offers services at the starting cost of $5.The name Fiverr is derived from an American Slang where, "Fiverr" actually means a five dollar bill. People from all over the world buy and sell services everyday on Fiverr.

The services offered in Fiver are numerous namely; advertisement, social networking and business promotion to translations, graphic designing and funny videos. These are just a few services that are offered on this awesome portal from other wide list of offerings. These offered services are also popularly known as "GIGS" on Fiverr. You can easily search for almost anything which you were looking for.

Fiverr has thousands of users; however, you don't need to worry about your data as it's totally secured and private. Fiverr is used globally by freelancers who offer different services to their clients. What a great site!

Fiverr charges 20% from transactions that are successful and if any transaction is not successful, Fiverr charges nothing. Nowadays, a lot of people make their living through Fiverr.

How to get started on Fiverr

A lot of persons don't really consider Fiverr as a serious source of income to make huge amount of money. If you are able to put in four to five hours of work each day, you are on your way to earning huge amount of money. There are top rated sellers on Fiverr who are actually making more than $3000 per month. You just need to work smart and harder, making sure you are familiar with some of the techniques that would help you in achieving your desired target.

How does this site work?

You just need to sign-up for free and become a service provider on this platform. You can easily become a service provider for a service you specialize in or have passion for. For all your transactions on Fiverr, you would be asked to link your Fiverr account with your PayPal account. Your buyers would be asked to first pre-pay $5 to Fiverr, before you can begin the work. Fiverr would then transfer this to your account upon completion of your work, and receiving a confirmation from your buyer that the work has been done. So, the chances of you getting cheated are very slim.

The commission Fiverr charged for this service is 20% of your revenue.

How to set-up a Fiverr account:

Below is a simple step by step instruction on how to set up your Fiverr account:

1. Visit https://www.fiverr.com/

2. Click on "Join" link on right hand top corner. You would be served with three optioned:

a. Create a new account using your email address

b. Connect using Facebook login credentials

c. Connect using Google login credentials

3. Click on an option and follow the instructions thereafter accordingly.

a. Immediately you accept the terms and conditions (if you logged in using Facebook or Google page) it would bring you back to a screen, where it would confirm your username and email ID.

b. Post validating both the credentials you may click on "Join" tab.

Now, you are ready to start using your account at Fiverr.

This platform is an outstanding place to validate your services, products, and ideas.

This would also help you to improve upon your sales skills as well.

If your Gigs are well prepared and meet the demand of clients, you can have a high and consistent earning potential. The following tips will help you run Fiverr business successfully:

1. Always be in constant touch with the buyers.

2. Make you clients happy,

3. Answer all the questions that they may have

4. Inspire them to leave positive feedback on your gigs and promote the same within their group.

Services that sells on Fiverr

People around the world looking for low cost services are attracted to this platform. On Fiverr, it is the owners of small businesses that are the main customers. They flood into the site looking for high quality work at affordable cost.

Buyers, who are in need of SEO (search engine optimization) services, should avoid buying gigs from this platform. It is widely known that SEO gigs from Fiverr don't portray businesses well.

What gigs should be purchased on Fiverr?

Introduction videos, graphic designing, product boxes, cover designs, ebooks and others gigs can be purchased on Fiverr. As a buyer, you should purchase only from a top rated seller.

Sellers on Fiverr are people who want to make extra money online. They put in more efforts to getting customers and giving out quality services. In case someone cheats you on this platform, you may contact Fiverr support team and they would take care of it from there. In situations that are serious, Fiverr would surely make a refund to you and the scammers are logged out.

How to earn money on this platform

You can make huge amount of money on this platform by offering high quality services that targets a certain niche. You need to know that any business requires time and a good amount of hard work, before it starts earning money. This holds true on this platform as well.

Turning this platform into a serious business

If you consider and see Fiverr as a serious business, then these small deposits of $5 can convert your PayPal account to $500 to $1000 every month. But, how do you actually make money from these $5 gigs?

1. Offer the services which do not take a lot of time to get completed

2. Offering services for fixing bugs for software or writing articles consume time and might not favour you here. Therefore, it wouldn't be advisable to invest on these kinds of gigs.

3. Making money on this platform is that simple. For example, to earn $800 every month, you need to make $15 every hour, which means 3 gigs in an hour, or every gig should only consume 20 minutes of your time or less.

4. There are only a few services which are easy and could help you earn Money fast, creation of timeline covers for a Facebook account, logo creation, video recording (20 -30 seconds), twitter followers, and this list is not an exhaustive list.

5. Always see yourself as the prospective buyer you offering your services to before deciding to sell a service.

How to drive traffic to your Fiverr gigs

1. The keywords used in your gigs play a very important role in Fiverr.

2. Make sure that appropriate keywords are included in your gig's title

3. It is important Keywords are included in your gig's description

4. Appropriate tagging should be done on your gigs

5. If possible, including a video describing the gig

6. Make eye-catching images that attract many visitors

7. Your gig should be publicized on appropriate forums threads.

8. Don't fail to share your gig on Twitter, Facebook etc.

9. Your descriptions should be concise and clear, preferably in bullet format.

10. Try to include testimonials from successfully completed gigs.

11. Make Basic SEO (search engine optimization) for your homepage

can route traffic straight from Google page for your services.

These are the few important tips you should keep in mind before creating a Fiverr business.

How to Build a Top Selling Fiverr Gig

We have gathered a few tips to create a top selling Fiverr Gig. Let's start with the basics.

How to Create a Gig?

1. On the top bar, click "Sales" tab

2. Now click on the "Create Gig" tab on the right side of the page

Few important tips to remember:

A Captivating Title

If you explain everything in the title it would make it look cluttered and may even cluster up the words in the link. Google Keyword Planner may help you search for good words to use in your title if you are confused of the words selection to use.

Choosing correct categories

For your gigs to stand out, place them in the correct category and subcategory. A gig that is related to shoes won't make any sense in the computer category. Also, make different gigs to suit the different categories.

Displaying images

Make sure that all the images of your gigs have been uploaded to the gig gallery. Always consider following pointers while uploading the images in this gallery:

Picture format should always be in .jpeg

Picture size should not be greater than 2MB

The size in pixels should be 682 (width) x459 (height)

It is important you should have the copyright of the image you are uploading.

Description

Your description provided should include all the possible information that is useful to the buyer. You can use bullet points to explain in details your services. Make sure your description should be limited to approximately 200 words or 1,200 characters only. Give room for creativity while you are formatting the description. You may even use text highlighter option to boost the description.

Tags and Keywords

You have the option of using up to five tags combining them with multiple keywords.

Your Video

The pointers you should remember while creating a video are:

The size should be less than 50 MB.

Video should be of a high quality or HD quality.

The length of the video should be in the range of 15 (not less) to 60 (not more) seconds only.

There should be an excellent statement, "Exclusive on Fiverr" either in text format or heard clearly.

You should have the copyright of all the images or footages or music you use in the video.

Note that all the videos are reviewed by the Fiverr team, before being made public.

Feedback

You may add a postscript in the delivery templates. Here, you can request the buyers to rate your gig as "thumbs up" if the gig was valuable. The drift in Fiverr says approximately 80% ratings for thumbs up, whereas the remaining 20% is not rated at all.

Time- Tested Fiverr Gigs

Every day new individuals are registering on Fiverr. Therefore, there is a very stiff competition on Fiverr. To make it easier for you, I have collated hot selling gigs you can start with.

1. Designing: Logos, Banners, Cartoons and Social Media

Graphic or Logo designing:

This is one of the simplest and best services to be offered on this platform. It is very quick and straightforward for someone to create a graphic if he is talented in graphic designing, photoshop and others. People can create more than 50 logos in approximately 4 hours, which is around $1000 in profits,

Banner ads:

You can find banners of much better quality at Fiverr compared to large design companies who charge you more than $30 for same service. People find the designers on this platform and create a long term relationship with them. If you mix this with log designing, than you have the potential to offer two of the best gigs to the buyers.

Cartoons:

If you have the ability to create cartoons of people, than you have the opportunity to access a large market.

Social media:

People often buy graphic designs for their Facebook, YouTube and Twitter pages like their Facebook fan page timeline cover photos. I even have a friend that purchased one for his Facebook fan page!

2. Video formation–Intro/Outro–Infographic Videos –Humorous Videos

If you have nice video controlling and editing software and can integrate effects into video, then you will be able to accomplish all of the above.

In **Intro/Outro** creation, once you get the after effects, you may look at some tutorials on YouTube and make some basic intro designs and sell them to people for $5. Once you have produced a video project it will take you one minute to add in the person's text, after that you just have to assemble the video and you will be good to go.

Infographic videos: They are currently in high demand and are simple to create. WSO Software is available online and you can purchase one that you can use to create infographic videos with a significantly lower amount of time.

You simply have to apply text and click on compile.

Humorous videos: Hot girls or strange men only. If you choose either of these categories then you will be able to create hilarious and funny videos for $5 or do something crazy for $5. You can hum happy birthday to somebody or you may even give them a sexy dance. Be Creative!

Controlling and Editing. The hardest task is for a YouTuber to editing videos daily. Editing is simply one of the fastest ways to profit using Fiverr. Provided that you've got speedy internet and superior editing software, you can have a consistent amount of buyers.

3. Voice Acting

Have a good quality microphone and use it with a radio voice to create a voice acting gig. Using a high quality microphone and a pop filter allows you to deliver studio quality sound to your Fiverr service.

If you want to earn on money you should probably start selling Voice acting. This is mainly because it's so straightforward to control and provided that you have got a high quality microphone, you will be able to do wonderful things in a short period of time.

4. Writing – Articles

If you are able to write up to 10,000 words per day, you can create a Fiverr writing gig which you can use for consistent profits.

Articles. People who are good in writing and quickly respond to requests do get offers of 50 + gigs from clients on Fiverr. There is a lot of money to be made in the article writing industry. You'll need twenty consistent and reliable clients to be able to earn a full wage from writing articles.

Sales copy. If you are actually an excellent copywriter and you are not interested in writing 10,000 to 20,000 thousand words per day then you can look into writing sales copy. This will include the things like sales videos, text on ads, sales pages and landing page text.

5. Quality check – Article Editing

Quality check and Proofreading of articles are another set of gig to do on Fiverr. Just a couple of proof readers exist on Fiverr. Numerous gigs use automated software to just confirm for spelling errors. People use proofreading for content flow and grammar, and not only for spelling.

This makes space in the market for people who enjoy proofreading and editing content. You can charge around $5.00 for $500 – 1000 words and maybe add $5 for every 1,000 words thereafter.

6. WordPress Problem Solving

If you can solve problems and errors with WordPress; then Fiverr is the right place to sell your service. WordPress problem solving gigs are constantly earning money. They sell loads of gigs and the jobs usually take a short period of time to complete depending on your prowess with Wordpress.

7. Business suggestion – Marketing suggestion

You can give guidance and suggestions on business, advertising and marketing on Fiverr. People are always happy to see what $5 can get for the advice on their business. Most people who give services like this have some pre-designed templates that they just use over and over again.

8. False Likes, supporters, Favourites & Shares

False social presence is a multi-million dollar industry that has been in the trend do to the boom in social media marketing. If you can get your hands on the correct software that creates and verifies Twitter and Facebook accounts, you can easily earn lots of money using Fiverr.

There are many programmes that create fake Twitter accounts that will follow anyone you tell them too. It can create thousands of Twitter accounts in a few minutes and you can tell them all to follow, like and share or re-tweet. This makes it easy to provide a service like this.

9. Shout Outs on Social Media

If you have a big Twitter, Facebook, Instagram or Tumblr following, you can offer shout-outs to your buyers. It only takes a matter of seconds to tweet a message to your audience and as far as your audience is made up of real people, buyers will keep coming back for more.

10. Marketing – Banner Ads –leaflets --Links.

You can also earn money by promoting people's business, websites social profiles and blogs using flyers, leaflets, banner ads and links.

How to Promote your Gigs on Fiverr

Once you setup and create a gig, you need these tips to know how to apply the secret sauce to your Fiverr gig:

Step 1 – Create a Dummy Account

You need to buy your gig twice. Make sure to give your gig a positive and remarkable review.

Step 2 – Forged Visitors

Now, you just need to send no less than two hundred and fifty fake hits/visitors to your Fiverr gig. This automatically increases your gigs impressions, making it noticeable to buyers. If you are not aware of how to get fake visitors, you can just purchase them from Fiverr; however do not go overboard with them.

Step 3 – Precise Tags

Make sure you use correct and precise tags for your gigs and also take account of the keywords you want to rank for in the heading title and description.

You can use tags like-

1. 3D animation

2. Whiteboard

3. Video animation

4. Whiteboard animation

Top Five Secrets to Becoming a Top Rated Seller on Fiverr:

Secret 1. You should not be rude to sellers who might have

overlooked your instructions.

Be humble, kind and courteous and remind the customer about their order and if they have missed anything in their order.

Secret 2. Receiving GREAT feedback and comments from buyers.

Give incentives and offers to your buyers to give you good feedback when you send your work. You may offer your client a free email course, a video tutorial or give them great value while you deliver your work. This will generate GREAT results and feedback.

Even if you don't receive any nice comment or feedback, you can still click the positive feedback button and say positive things like "Wow, thanks for the work. I appreciate the gig. Happy to work for you again."

Remember that new Buyers will be examining your work, and if they see row after row of Orders Completed, you will attract the buyer much more because there is already a proven track record.

Secret 3. Handling Negative Feedback.

Converse with the buyer and politely suggest you jointly cancel the job and refund with a promise that the buyer removes the negative remark. Be practical and tell them you have misunderstood the task and you'd be happy to do it over again.

You can clear the bad remark through delivery of more quality refined work you deliver to your clients.

Secret 4. Keep in mind that Buyers Judge a Book by its Cover

Attractive shiny things get clicks. The dull and dreary looking Gigs will simply get overlooked. If your gig looks plain, then don't expect a lot of Buyers knocking on your door. Understand that if your graphics skills are not so hot, then you need to find a Fiverr freelancer with killer graphics skills.

Secret 5. Ask for the help of Fiverr Editors

To boost visibility, ask for help from editors on Fiverr platform. This will show up your gig a little higher on the first page.

Follow these Steps to Get Started

Here are some great steps that you can do to start on your Fiverr success journey right away!

Step - I: Connect to Fiverr.com

Register and create a profile on Fiverr to boost your online presence on the site, and also get you recognized by buyers. Choose an effective name and add a striking profile image. The third task is to add a description - who you are, how you can help others and why your services are different from others.

Step - II: Establish Some Gigs

Launch three to five gigs on Fiverr and get ready to work as buyers will come. Once more, another secret trick is to make use of tags when you post your new gigs.

Step - III: Reply to Requests

Aim to reply as many requests as possible without spamming, or you may get banned. You can even copy-paste your offers making some simple customization or you can forward them to your gig links.

Step - IV: Make Reputation

Try and maintain a clean reputation by delivering quality jobs and on time to avoid negative comments.

Step - V: Leverage other platforms

To be sincere, you can sell most of the stuff you buy on Fiverr.com for at least 2 to 3 times higher than prices on other platforms. Find other platforms like oDesk or glance to get more leads and more buyers.

Step - VI: Have several accounts

This can really be helpful if you want to focus on some special services through one account and something else using the other. This could help if you have some negative ratings on one of the accounts.

CONCLUSION

Pick Your Cash Cow!

I am excited now you have known the five proven ways to earn make money online every month, and I know you are going to ACT NOW and not wait. Remember, procrastination is the thief of time. Your TOMORROW begins NOW.

Let's summarize your "Proven Money Making Strategies" procedure:

- •• Blogging for money
- •• Article Writing that Sells
- •• Profiting with eBay
- •• Craigslist to Profits
- •• Take advantage of YouTube
- •• Fiverr Money Secrets

Now that you know these 6 money making strategies, **there is still one thing left for you to do: Choose one.**

Don't struggle over this decision. The reason is because these are all proven ways to make you make money online.

From the list, the "best" one is easy to spot. The one that suits your lifestyle is the one that will bring you the most profit!

WISH YOU BEST OF LUCK.

ABOUT THE AUTHOR

Bassey Jimmy is a businessman, writer, and an Internet marketing expert. He is the president of *Believe Marketing Inc.* and the author of many other books to list here, including *3 Things You Need To Make $1000 Monthly.*

He left banking nine years ago and since then has taken the internet by storm.

Mr. Jimmy is happily married with four lovely children.

www.ingramcontent.com/pod-product-compliance
Lightning Source LLC
Chambersburg PA
CBHW061200180526
45170CB00002B/887